THE
FUTURE
OF
ARCHITECTURE
100
BUILDINGS

BY
MARC KUSHNER

EDITED BY JENNIFER KRICHELS

TED Books
Simon & Schuster

London   New York   Toronto   Sydney   New Delhi

TEDBooks

First published in Great Britain by Simon & Schuster UK Ltd, 2015
A CBS COMPANY

First TED Books hardcover edition March 2015

TED, the TED logo, and TED Books are trademarks of
TED Conferences, LLC.

For information on licensing the TED talk that accompanies this
book, or other content partnerships with TED, please contact
TEDBOOKS@TED.COM.

3 5 7 9 10 8 6 4 2

Simon & Schuster UK Ltd
1st Floor
222 Gray's Inn Road
London WC1X 8HB

www.simonandschuster.co.uk

Simon & Schuster Australia, Sydney
Simon & Schuster India, New Delhi

A CIP catalogue record for this book is available
from the British Library

ISBN: 978-1-47114-176-8
ISBN: 978-1-47114-177-5 (ebook)

Interior design by MGMT
Jacket Design by Lewis Csizmazia

Printed and bound by CPI Group (UK) Ltd, Croydon, CR0 4YY

EXTREME LOCATIONS

REINVENTION

GET BETTER

CONTENTS

POP-UP

45

46

46

47

48

SHAPE-SHIFTERS

52

54

55

56

58

58

60

62

63

64

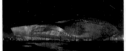
66

67

69

69

70

71

72

74

75

DRIVE

77

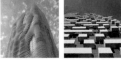
77

78

80

NATURE BUILDING

80 81 82 87 87

89 90 91 92 94

SHELTER FROM THE STORM

94 97 97 100 102

103 104 106 109 109

SHRINK

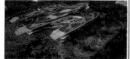

110 112 114 114 115

SOCIAL CATALYSTS

116 117 120 121 123 123

CONTENTS

THE
FUTURE
OF
ARCHITECTURE
IN
100
BUILDINGS

Introduction

This book wants you to ask more from architecture.

You live in a house, you work in an office, you send your kids to a school. These places aren't just the backdrop to your life, they shape your life—they define who you see, what you see, and how you see it.

Architecture impacts how you feel every day, which isn't surprising considering how much time we all spend inside buildings. The average American, for example, spends 90 percent of their time indoors, yet so many of our buildings leave us without natural light, shelter us with low ceilings, and ignore our personal, social, and environmental needs.

It doesn't have to be like this. We can control this powerful force—we just have to start asking more from our buildings.

This architectural revolution is already upon us. The average person is more comfortable having an opinion about architecture today than ever before, mostly due to the dialogue enabled by social media. The world's 1.75 billion smartphones are fundamentally changing the way architecture is consumed, turning everyone into an architectural photographer. Photographs shared on social media liberate buildings from their geographic locations, enabling a new level of public engagement. We experience architecture today with an unprecedented immediacy, creating fodder for a global conversation about buildings and their impact.

This communications revolution is making us all comfortable critiquing the built environment around us, even if that criticism is just "OMG I luv this!" or "This place gives me the creeps." This feedback is removing architecture from the exclusive purview of experts and critics and putting power into the hands of the people who matter: everyday users. We have started "liking" and hating places out loud. Architects can hear us in real time, which has empowered (and sometimes even forced) them to pursue new ideas—to create solutions that respond to today's most pressing social and environmental issues.

In this new world, one in which people are asking more from their buildings, architects are no longer bound by any single style at any single time. People don't want their town library in Seattle to look the same as their grandmother's library in New Jersey. Even architectural historians don't know exactly what is going on right now because everything is changing so fast. In fact, they will never know what is going on again, because the future of architecture is a frenetic whirlwind of experimentation and a reevaluation of long-accepted habits.

This book considers the public to be a partner in architecture. The questions we can ask of buildings, and of architects, will create a new future—one that will look a lot different than the world we know today. Some of the questions this book poses may seem silly: What if a cow built your house? Can we swim in poop? Can we live on the moon? But two hundred years ago it was wild to ask, Will I live in the sky? Or, Will I need a sweater in the summer? Now that elevators and air conditioning enable us to live in the clouds and freeze in a heat wave, we must ask harder, more imaginative questions.

Architects have the know-how to design buildings that are greener, smarter, and friendlier—and now the public is a partner in this ambition. In one hundred examples, this book is a primer on how you and I and the entire world can ask for good architecture.

How we chose these buildings

The more than one hundred projects chosen for this book are a nonscientific and purely subjective collection of the most interesting and relevant work being done in the field of architecture. They represent every continent in the world and multiple building types. They are big and small, conceptual and concrete. They were initially culled from more than five thousand Architizer A+ Awards entries and supplemented by exhaustive research, conversations, and personal experience.

EXTREME LOCATIONS

Humankind's desire to explore and build in extreme locations raises a crucial question: How? How will scientists survive when they settle at the North Pole? How will naturalists take shelter when they observe reindeer in the Norwegian tundra? How will our children live when they land on Mars?

1 Can we live in the harshest place on Earth?

Forget outer space—scientists are still navigating uncharted territories here on Earth. This relocatable research facility sits on the Brunt Ice Shelf at the southernmost Antarctic station, operated by the British Antarctic Survey. Perched on giant ski-like foundations, hydraulic legs allow the station to "climb" out of the snow after heavy precipitation; when the ice shelf moves out to sea in warmer weather, modules can be lowered onto skis and towed to a new location. Setting a new bar for climate change research in the polar regions, its spaceship-like form draws much-deserved attention to this groundbreaking work.

Your survival depends on good design.

Halley VI Antarctic Research Station. Antarctica
HUGH BROUGHTON ARCHITECTS AND AECOM, CONSTRUCTED BY GALLIFORD TRY FOR THE BRITISH ANTARCTIC SURVEY

2 What does architecture look like above 10,000 feet?

Accessible only by gondola, this Austrian ski lodge sits 11,000 feet above sea level. It is designed to work with the natural landscape's sheer visual and physical power; the structure is perched on the mountain's summit to enable nature's unique "snow architecture" to accumulate and melt unimpeded. An abundance of glass windows allows for nearly 360-degree views, framed by a specially engineered floor and roof designed to withstand the elements and huge temperature swings of the setting.

Wildspitzbahn.
Tirol, Austria
BAUMSCHLAGER
HUTTER PARTNERS

Nature is the ultimate architect.

3 Can architecture be a path into the clouds?

These viewing platforms hover above the Trollstigen road, a mountainous tourist path that twists and turns up near-vertical slopes and perches on a dramatic pass between Norway's deep fjords. Humans may only visit—and build—there in the summer, when the weather is less harsh, but the platforms must withstand weather conditions year-round. Though the route delicately threads through the treacherous terrain, it relies on remarkable strength and careful engineering to stand the test of Norway's harsh elements.

Trollstigen National
Tourist Route.
Trollstigen, Norway
REIULF RAMSTAD
ARKITEKTER

The best architecture makes us forget how hard it works.

4 What do reindeer do all day?

A hiking trail leads to a spectacular site over-looking the Dovrefjell mountain range in central Norway, home to some of the last remaining wild reindeer herds in Europe. A sinewy pavilion invites visitors to warm themselves while observing the local reindeer population. The structure is an exercise in mate-rial contrast—a rigid outer shell of raw steel and glass houses a soft wooden core shaped like the nearby rocks, which have been eroded by winds and running water for centuries.

Architecture rewards the adventurous.

Tverrfjellhytta —
Norwegian Wild
Reindeer Pavilion.
Hjerkinn, Norway
SNØHETTA

5 Can modern architecture inspire pilgrimage?

The Ruta del Peregrino is a pilgrimage route that winds 72 miles through the Jalisco mountain range. Nearly two million people each year make the arduous walk to honor the Virgin of Talpa. This lookout point is one of nine pieces of architecture designed to provide landmarks and shelter for these travelers (and attract more casual visitors to the route as well). Balanced like a seesaw, it frames the view at one of the highest points on the trail and offers a moment of respite from the trail's harsh conditions.

Architecture can make the journey.

Ruta del Peregrino
Crosses Lookout Point.
Jalisco mountains,
Mexico
ELEMENTAL

6 Can you dream beneath the Northern Lights?

This luxury hotel uses Iceland's otherworldly landscape to create a completely escapist experience for guests. The architects chose the location very carefully—local lore discourages disturbing cave-dwelling elves nearby. With the environment in mind, the architects made ample use of recycled materials; rubber tires were remade into bathroom basins and lava into lamps. A nearly infinite, yet sustainable, supply of hot water comes from a 190-degrees-Celsius hot spring heated by a nearby volcano. And when nighttime comes, the heavens above put on a show like none other.

Architecture reveals outer space on our own planet.

ION Luxury
Adventure Hotel.
Thingvellir National
Park, Iceland
MINARC

7 Can a building stand on tiptoe?

At this desolate resort, the cabins are designed to encourage inhabitants to appreciate the isolation of the desert. Rather than planting each 20-square-meter EcoLoft hotel room on the ground like a traditional building, the architects designed them to hover over the land on thin steel supports. They are arranged like the boulders around the site, scattered in a picturesque composition.

Ecotourism needs ecoarchitecture.

Encuentro Guadalupe.
Baja California, Mexico
GRACIA STUDIO

8 Can an office float?

The Arctia Shipping Ltd. headquarters is a floating office building whose design references its neighbors: icebreaking barges docked on the Katajanokka shore, built to combat the building's extremely low temperatures. Its horizontal mass and customized black steel facades mimic the black hulls of the ships, while interior finishes of lacquered wood recall earlier shipbuilding traditions.

If buildings can float, whole cities could too.

Arctia Shipping
Headquarters.
Helsinki, Finland
K2S ARCHITECTS

9 Can a landscraper help us reach the stars?

In the Chilean Atacama Desert sits the Very Large Telescope, an instrument that's true to its name—it's one of the largest and most advanced pieces of optical equipment on Earth. At this flagship facility, operated by the European Southern Observatory, scientists working in severe climatic conditions (intense sun, extreme dryness, earthquakes) need lodging that will help them rest and recover between work shifts. This hotel is draped across the landscape, and has become a respite for those making extended visits to this beautiful, harsh environment.

Scientific progress requires healthy scientists.

European Southern
Observatory
(ESO) Hotel.
Cerro Paranal, Chile
AUER WEBER

10 Can we live on the moon?

When we all eventually live on the moon, we'll need to be protected from gamma radiation. This four-person dwelling will do just that, providing shelter from huge temperature swings and meteorites. Inflatable domes give the structure its unique shape. Robots powered by solar energy will 3-D print moon dust (regolith) onto its surface, creating a protective shell that is ultralightweight because it requires no glue or other fasteners—its particles bond together naturally. Architects have created a 1.5-ton mock-up and have tested small modules inside a vacuum chamber. Look for the first structure soon at the moon's south pole.

Architectural ingenuity isn't earthbound.

3-D printed lunar habitations. (Concept)
FOSTER + PARTNERS WITH THE EUROPEAN SPACE AGENCY

REINVENTION

It's bad enough to throw out a plastic bottle—imagine throwing out a whole building when you're done with it! New construction is wildly inefficient, which is why, for example, 90 percent of construction activity in the United States over the next ten years is expected to be on existing buildings. A grain silo becomes an art museum, and a water treatment plant becomes an icon. We can create a new future for our existing buildings by repurposing our past.

11 Can you shop in a cathedral?

As the number of brick-and-mortar bookstores in the world dwindles, the ones that remain have become sacred places to retreat. So what better place for a Dutch bookseller to reimagine itself than inside a thirteenth-century Dominican cathedral? The soaring nave allows ample space for a three-story-high bookshelf, which spans the length of the space and contrasts with the Gothic stone architecture around it.

Retail therapy can be a holy experience.

Selexyz Dominicanen.
Maastricht, Netherlands
EVELYNE MERKX,
MERKX + GIROD

12 Can rubble tell a new story?

Rubble from natural disasters is reborn, fittingly, as a history museum in China. Architects used the debris accumulated through earthquakes to build the facade of this building, commissioned by the city of Ningbo. Built in this way, the architects' vision becomes an icon of the past while advancing sustainable ideas of adapting existing materials to contemporary needs.

Bricks don't have an expiration date.

Ningbo Museum.
Ningbo, China
WANG SHU

13 Can ugly be pretty?

Newtown Creek is the largest of **New York City's** fourteen wastewater treatment plants. The city could have easily stuck with a utilitarian design, but instead it decided to put **$4.5 billion** into overhauling the outmoded and environmentally unsound wastewater treatment facility, following a design that is sensitive to the surrounding residential neighborhood. Working with a team that included lighting artists and an environmental sculptor, the architects created a complex that uses form, material, and color to create a striking visual composition.

Industrial architecture doesn't need to hide anymore.

Newtown Creek
Wastewater
Treatment Plant.
Brooklyn, New York,
United States
ENNEAD ARCHITECTS

14 Would you eat dinner in a sewer pipe?

Just try not to think about it—stacked precast concrete pipes traditionally used for wastewater become a dramatic, sculptural addition to an existing pub. Lined with wood, they create intimate dining nooks for those inside, and a sense of voyeurism for those who pass by.

Function follows form.

Prahran Hotel.
Melbourne, Australia
TECHNÉ ARCHITECTS

15 How much would you pay to sleep in a warehouse?

Repurposing warehouses into trendy hotels is happening around the globe—but this is a particularly striking instance of updated architecture bringing new life to a formerly industrial setting. On the East River in Brooklyn, the architects stripped and restored a brick, cast iron, and timber-frame building to create seventy-three guest rooms. A roof addition smartly uses contextual factory windows to create panoramic views of the Manhattan skyline while forming a visible icon on Brooklyn's own skyline.

Rest easy knowing you're cooler than everyone else.

Wythe Hotel.
Brooklyn, New York, United States
MORRIS ADJMI ARCHITECTS

16 How do you turn a grain silo into an art museum?

A historic grain silo composed of forty-two concrete tubes will become a museum on Cape Town's waterfront. The structure had no open space to begin with, so architects cut a cross section through eight of the central concrete silos (new concrete-cutting techniques will preserve their edges and add texture to the space). The effect is an oval atrium encircled by concrete shafts on every side. Artists will have the chance to create site-specific art in the silo's original underground tunnels.

Zeitz Museum of Contemporary Art Africa.
Cape Town, South Africa
HEATHERWICK STUDIO

A building can go from feeding mouths to feeding minds.

17 Can a bunker become a power plant?

In the landmark ruins of the World War Two-era Hamburg-Wilhelmsburg flak bunker, a drastic reimagining of the structure's purpose has taken place. It's now a green machine that converts heat to energy and almost wipes out its own carbon footprint. But its history hasn't been forgotten—located in the middle of a residential area, the bunker is also publically accessible as a memorial with a café.

Energy Bunker.
Hamburg, Germany
HHS PLANER
+ ARCHITEKTEN

Architecture reminds us that our memories are powerful.

18 Can superhighways make good houses?

We have all driven on highways without realizing their enormousness. This house awakens us to the scale of our transportation infrastructure. It's made using huge precast concrete beams that are traditionally fabricated for highway construction. A series of seemingly impossible cantilevers make us rethink our perceptions of gravity and scale. And check out that swimming pool!

Rethinking the obvious can create something entirely new.

Hemeroscopium House.
Madrid, Spain
ENSAMBLE STUDIO

19 Can a new skin save old bones?

When developers looked to transform a 1960s hotel into a high-end apartment building, their architects wanted to save as much of the building as possible while still upgrading its performance and overall image. They did this by creating a "second skin" for the building, which they installed onto the existing masonry facade. The new black aluminum panels host a vertical garden and drastically improve the thermal performance of the building (and look great doing it).

Good for the environment can be good for the eyes.

142 Park Street.
South Melbourne,
Australia
BRENCHLEY ARCHITECTS

20 Can historic cities have futuristic public spaces?

When Seville decided to replace the parking lot and bus station at its city center, officials were surprised to discover Roman ruins beneath the surface. What to do? Metropol Parasol was the winning scheme in an international competition that manages to protect the ruins, provide space for shopping and cafés, and create a grand new public square for the still-vibrant city. The six mushroomlike shading devices provide relief from the intense Andalusian sun, and visitors can climb to the top to take in a panoramic view of the walled city. Yet the craziest part of this swoopy landmark isn't its form: It is made mostly of wood and is the largest glued structure on Earth.

Cities are not time capsules.

Metropol Parasol.
Seville, Spain
J. MAYER H.

21 Can a subway station make you want to be underground?

This Budapest subway station extension was planned during the 1980s, but wasn't implemented until the new millennium. New construction techniques allowed the architects to excavate a giant box shape and use concrete beams to structure it. The haptic collection of columns, beams, and escalators is illuminated by the sun through a glass ceiling, making this subterranean space feel like a three-dimensional traffic intersection and transforming it into a valued public space.

Good architecture is worth the wait.

M4 Fővám tér and Szent Gellért tér stations. Budapest, Hungary SPORAARCHITECTS

22 Can shipping containers be surprising?

Shipping containers—uniform in size, low in cost, available everywhere—offer an appealing building block for architects. Built to attract visitors to the Anyang waterfront's public art program, the APAP OpenSchool pushes the boundaries of what these modules can do. With one container skewed at a seemingly impossible 45-degree angle and another hovering 3 meters above the ground, the structure becomes a landmark within the city with the help of some bright yellow paint.

Architecture can invent extraordinary uses for ordinary materials.

APAP OpenSchool.
Anyang, Korea
LOT-EK

23 Can good architecture make 1+2=1?

The Museu de Arte do Rio and its adjacent school had an identity problem. The institutions are composed of three buildings: a 1910 palace, a midcentury bus station, and a former police hospital building. To create a single identity, the architects created a hovering concrete canopy to visually unite the disparate pieces. Thanks to barely-visible columns, the wave-like canopy seems to float over the museum campus, a bustling rooftop plaza, and the courtyard below.

With the right design, architecture can be more than the sum of its parts.

Museu de Arte do Rio.
Rio de Janeiro, Brazil
JACOBSEN ARQUITETURA

GET BETTER

Buildings impact our health and well-being. If you've ever felt depressed while sitting in a waiting room with low ceilings and harsh, flickering fluorescent lights, then you know the power of architecture over our psyches. The inverse is true too: buildings can have a hugely positive impact on the people who depend on them, from medical patients and doctors to students and the elderly.

24 Can a brick become a healing force?

In 2011, Butaro Hospital opened a 150-bed medical facility that serves nearly 350,000 people in this region of Rwanda. In spite of its impact, the hospital struggled to attract doctors to work there. The solution came in the form of these charming doctors' homes, which give foreign staff a permanent residence just five minutes from the hospital. In building the homes, architects took a truly holistic view of the community's needs and used the project as an opportunity to teach new skilled trades to the local community. On-site workshops taught

local teams to make compressed stabilized
earth blocks—bricks that are earthquake-safe
and sustainable. These teams also learned
to make the hospital's custom furniture and
light fixtures, as well as the earth-stabilizing
landscaping techniques crucial to bringing
agriculture to the region. With a total of nine
hundred skilled laborers trained during the
construction process, the effort brought better
building practices, not to mention better medi-
cine, to Rwanda for generations to come.

Buildings build futures.

Butaro Doctors'
Housing,
Butaro, Rwanda
MASS DESIGN GROUP

25 What can a spa teach us about light?

A distinctive hotel built in 1967 has become a mainstay on the island of Majorca. Its latest renovation includes a new spa—one that relies on an innovative natural lighting design to completely transform the interior spaces. In the pool area, the building can finally take advantage of its sunniest facade via a roof and walls punctuated by arrays of strategically placed windows. In the spa rooms and workout area, huge glass windows let guests see the landscape, whereas smaller openings create a dark, serene environment in quiet areas like the sauna.

Sunlight can be a transformative experience.

Hotel Castell dels Hams.
Majorca, Spain
A2ARQUITECTOS

26 Would you die here?

This unique housing complex for the elderly reflects Portugal's cultural emphasis on quality of life. The human component is crucial in each piece of the design, which is based on a Mediterranean town—streets, plazas, and gardens are an extension of each residence. Translucent roofs light up as the evening falls, to ensure that elderly residents can move freely at night. This lighting scheme also becomes crucial in an emergency: triggering an alarm inside the house changes the roof light from white to red, signaling the need for help.

Light sends a message.

Alcabideche Social Complex.
Alcabideche, Portugal
GUEDES CRUZ ARCHITECTS

27 Can architecture help fight cancer?

A cancer-counseling center creates a microcommunity for visitors, caregivers, and counselors. With a jagged roofline that clearly distinguishes it from other hospital buildings nearby, the center is made up of seven small houses encircling two grassy courtyards. Here, patients and their families can learn, eat, exercise, and rest close to the main cancer ward, fostering close

collaboration between the hospital staff and the Danish Cancer Society. Functioning like a small community within the surrounding neighborhood, the center highlights the vital role that human contact can play in the treatment process.

Architecture can give a healing touch.

Livsrum.
Næstved, Denmark
EFFEKT

28 Can architecture give us superpowers?

The secret of longevity? Intergenerational contact, constant physical activity, social interaction, fun, and happiness. All of these attributes are embedded in the Fun House— the centerpiece of the progressive aging community in Palm Springs. Key to this building is Madeline Gins's trailblazing theory of "Reverse Destiny": using structures to challenge physical and mental capacities, and viewing architecture as a key ingredient to a longer and healthier life.

Architecture can keep us young.

Reversible Destiny Healing Fun House. (Concept) Palm Springs, California, United States ARAWAKA+GINS, REVERSIBLE DESTINY FOUNDATION

29 Can this school help autistic children learn?

This school is designed for students with autism spectrum disorder—students whose elevated senses can trigger traumatic responses to sudden transitions between physical spaces, as well as to large, undefined spaces. Nine residences and three classroom buildings are arranged to foster a therapeutic environment by allowing students to move gradually through the campus. Change in direction is signaled by soft turns rather than abrupt angles, slowly leading students to the doorway of each building.

Architecture can create beautiful choreography.

Center for Discovery.
Harris, New York,
United States
TURNER BROOKS
ARCHITECT

30 Can mud keep us safe?

Mae Tao Clinic is a humanitarian organization that provides free medical treatment, shelter, and food for more than three thousand children. Located a few miles from the Burmese border, the clinic needed to expand to make room for its increasing numbers. Members of this growing community built a new facility with local wood and adobe (mud bricks), which have been used as a weather- and fireproof building material in Thailand for centuries. Now, the new center is host to a healthcare education program that will create an even stronger social fabric in this border region.

Dirt can be the tie that binds.

New training center campus & temporary dormitories.
Mae Mo, Thailand
A.GOR.A ARCHITECTS

31 Would your kids visit you here?

Getting old shouldn't mean living in isolation. This home for the elderly is a hybrid of a hotel and a forward-thinking hospital. Each white cube apartment on the facade has a projecting balcony designed to shade windows below from harsh sun. This privacy is offset by the great public space the building is arranged around: The long building is a meandering path (you can literally walk on the roof) that surrounds a public courtyard where patients can gather and make new friends.

Buildings know there is strength in numbers.

House for elderly people.
Alcácer do Sal
Residences, Portugal
AIRES MATEUS

POP-UP

Scientists have laboratories. Architects have pop-ups.
These temporary structures are tiny experiments in form and space.

Can architecture pop-up?

Off-the-shelf acrylic tubes are assembled to create a rigid pavilion whose shape is inspired by a rough gemstone.

Bulgari Art Pavilion.
Manarat Al Saadiyat, Abu Dhabi, United Arab Emirates
NOT A NUMBER ARCHITECTS

Designed with emerging chefs and food truck culture in mind, a lightweight, corrugated plastic shell can expand to accommodate dinners for two or fifty.

PDU (Portable Dining Unit).
San Francisco, California, United States
EDG

A temporary floating wedding pavilion barely touches the ground, thanks to a balloon canopy filled with helium and draped in diaphanous fabric.

Floatastic.
New Haven, Connecticut, United States
QASTIC LABS

A temporary social hub on Governors Island at the Figment arts festival is made of 53,780 recycled bottles—the amount thrown away in New York City every hour.

Head in the Clouds.
Governors Island, New York, United States
STUDIO KLIMOSKI CHANG ARCHITECTS

Designers give a standard white party tent a makeover with a suspended landscape of white vinyl tubes.

Drift pavilion for Design Miami/2012.
Miami Beach, Florida, United States
SNARKITECTURE

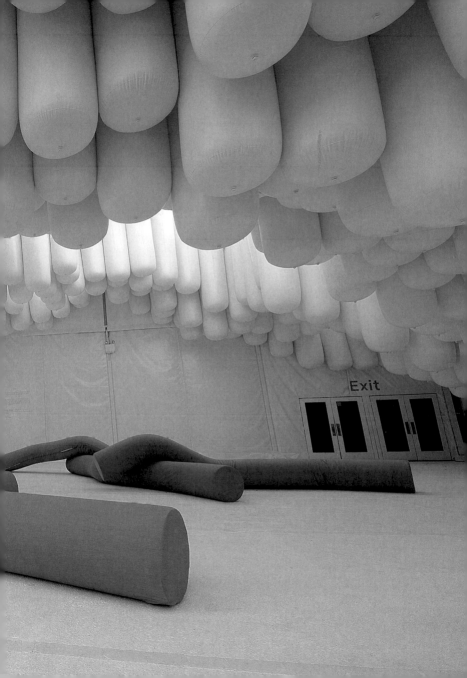

SHAPE
SHIFTERS

Can walls be invisible? Can a concert hall be a balloon? Can a skyscraper bend over and touch the ground? New technology for drawing, digital modeling, and construction means that architects are no longer bound by the shapes of the past, and can create unique spaces that look unlike anything we've seen before.

32 Can a building zig?

A border crossing is the first thing you encounter in a country, and the last thing you see as you leave. Georgia has built what must be the most interesting border crossing in the world, which is no surprise—since it was reborn as an independent democratic country in 1991, Georgia has been using architecture to rebrand its image to the world. Cantilevered platforms allow for viewing of the rugged landscape, and a cafeteria, conference room, and staff facilities are arranged to create a composition that promises wonderful discoveries in the country beyond.

The gateway to a country should entice and inspire visitors.

Border checkpoint.
Sarpi, Georgia
J. MEYER H. ARCHITECTS

33 Can architecture swirl?

An inflatable and mobile concert hall made of a stretchy plastic membrane brings both art and hope to earthquake-devastated Japan. The five-hundred-seat venue can inflate in under two hours and, when deflated, can move to a new location on the back of a truck.

The line between art and architecture can be a curvy one.

Ark Nova.
Matsushima, Japan
ARATA ISOZAKI,
ANISH KAPOOR

34 Can architecture swoop?

The Soviet Union was well known for its impos-
ing and rigidly monumental architecture. When
Azerbaijanis looked to create a new cultural
center in their capital, they made an extreme
departure from precedent. The building rises
out of the landscape in a series of undulating
curves to enclose over 57,000 square meters
of space. The design represents the fluid rela-
tionship between the city and what happens
inside the cultural center.

Heydar Aliyev Center.
Baku, Azerbaijan
ZAHA HADID ARCHITECTS

Architecture can create new landscapes.

35 Can architecture drip?

An international airport is an opportunity for a city to showcase its identity to visitors. That's why the architects of Terminal 2 in Mumbai's airport chose to reference the patterns of local jali window screens along its 17-acre roof. (*Jali* is the term for a perforated stone or latticed screen, usually with an ornamental pattern, often found in Indian architecture.) The coffered ceiling's pattern that drips into columns lets in light from above with skylights, creating a strong visual gateway to the nation's capital.

Architecture lets you know you've arrived.

Chhatrapati Shivaji
International Airport
Terminal 2.
Mumbai, India
SKIDMORE, OWINGS & MERRILL

36 Do buildings wear stockings?

In historic neighborhoods, new buildings should strike a balance between past and present architecture. For a new gallery in the northern part of Seoul, the architects created a white box that was ideal for the art inside, but too rigid-looking within its historic surroundings. A little wardrobe change did the trick: Wrapped in a flexible chain mail veil, the white box changes as light plays across its surface, better blending in with neighboring buildings.

Kukje Gallery.
Seoul, South Korea
SOLID OBJECTIVES-
IDENBURG LIU

A well-dressed building is never out of place.

37 Can architecture be from outer space?

The quiokly growing city of Dalian asked architects to create a functioning conference and opera center, but also a visual landmark for the city—something that could become an icon for the local community and excite an international audience. The result is almost entirely self-referential, as if an alien ship landed on the banks of Dalian's port. The building doesn't look to context for its reference, it looks to the future. It's a hopeful symbol of what the city will become: a place activated by visitors, commerce, and culture.

Dalian International
Conference Center.
Dalian, China
COOP HIMMELB(L)AU

Architecture doesn't predict the future, it creates the future.

38   What if an office building turned inside out?

Office design can be hard. Columns and pipes often get in the way of the much-vaunted "open-plan" design that, in turn, can get in the way of cubicles and conference rooms. Not so at O-14, an office tower that relies on a white concrete bearing wall three feet away from the windows to carry the building's load. That means there are no columns in the space. The structural wall creates a chimney effect that pulls hot air away from the building (good in the Dubai heat), and with 1,326 holes in five different shapes arranged artfully along the building's length, it makes an elegant state-ment about this new type of skyscraper design.

A hole new way of looking at structure.

O-14.
Dubai, United Arab Emirates
REISER + UMEMOTO

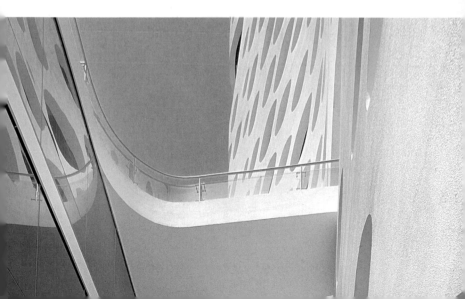

39 Can glitz be more than glam?

When this 40-year-old villa was transformed into apartments, it was at risk of losing its singular visual identity. To retain its identity and upgrade it for better environmental performance, architects installed a reflective outer wall in front of the existing building. This mirrored wall protects the building from the harsh sun, while unifying the apartments behind a single, continuous material—one that reflects the beautiful landscape.

Mirror, mirror, be the wall.

Trevox Apartments.
Naucalpan, Mexico
CRAFT ARQUITECTOS

40   Is pretty a public amenity?

In case you were wondering, this shape is called a rotated rhomboid. Clad in sixteen thousand hexagonal tiles, this Rodin sculpture museum's muscular structure is wrapped in a shimmering mirrored skin. The pattern references Mexico City's traditional colonial ceramic-tiled building facades and, like those buildings, changes in appearance with weather and the viewer's vantage point, becoming a sculpture itself.

A museum can be as important as the art within.

Museo Soumaya.
Mexico City, Mexico
FR-EE / FERNANDO
ROMERO ENTERPRISE

41 Can architecture be an Olympic sport?

Ski jumping is a death-defying sport; athletes risk life and limb to launch themselves impossibly high into the air. The village of Holmenkollen, in Norway, has been home to the most legendary jumps of the last century, and a recent international competition aimed to raise its reputation even higher with a new sports

campus and jumping hill. Clad in stainless steel mesh and cantilevered 226 feet, the ski jump is the longest of its kind, making sure it is always the center of attention.

Architecture gives you wings.

Holmenkollen Ski Jump.
Oslo, Norway
JDS ARCHITECTS

42 Can architecture be pixelated?

A building that's a simple cube is complicated by a facade of square panels in ten colors—just like a pixelated image. The playful design breaks down the form of the office, but it also performs the serious task of concealing the proprietary research and development conducted by the technology company within.

Architecture can keep secrets.

Frog Queen.
Graz, Austria
SPLITTERWERK

43 Can stone flow like a river?

Inspired by the geomorphology of the Louisiana region's ancient riverbed, this museum's sculptural foyer uses 1,100 cast stone panels to form a pathway to the museum's interior galleries. The panels were designed and assembled using a custom automation process.

Technology is the new alchemy, turning rocks into water.

Louisiana State Museum and Sports Hall of Fame. Natchitoches, Louisiana, United States
TRAHAN ARCHITECTS

44 Have we been thinking about windows all wrong?

The French call it a *brise soleil* ("sun breaker"). In Eastern architecture, it's a *muxarabi*. Wooden screens have a universal appeal for their dramatic appearance and serious sun-shading ability in hot weather. At a residence in São Paulo, two huge wooden curtains shelter the home of a young family, letting air flow through and creating a private enclave amid other houses. The best part is the mystery of this seemingly "windowless" house.

Every element of architecture is ripe for innovation.

BT House.
São Paolo, Brazil
STUDIO GUILHERME
TORRES

45 Why can't walls be invisible?

This is a museum for a glass collection, and the architects decided that a building for glass should be made of glass. The building is composed of a solid floor and a solid ceiling that appear to magically float on glass walls.

The boldest architecture is sometimes hard to see.

Glass Pavilion at the
Toledo Museum of Art.
Toledo, Ohio, United States
SANAA

46 Can a library be a mountain?

The illiteracy rate in the Netherlands town of Spijkenisse is a whopping 10 percent, so the city launched a type of architectural public relations campaign for books. Near the town square, community, educational, and commercial spaces were stacked into a pyramid, then wrapped with a 480-meter-long bookcase. Glass facades expose the library's collection, inviting everyone who passes to come inside.

Familiar buildings can still surprise us.

Stichting Openbare Bibliotheek.
Spijkenisse, Netherlands
MVRDV

47 Does a building need to be tall to change the skyline?

In Europe, residential buildings surround courtyards; in Manhattan, they reach for the sky. West 57th is the best of both worlds: its walls create a sheltered green space for occupants while maintaining the sweeping city vantage point offered by a skyscraper. Rising to a 450-foot peak, the building's shape lets sunlight deep into the block while keeping views of the Hudson River open for neighbors.

A condo tower doesn't need to be inward looking (and it doesn't need to be a tower).

West 57th.
New York, New York,
Unites States
ARCHITECT: WINKA
DUBBELDAM,
ARCHI-TECTONICS
CREATOR AND DIRECTOR:
RODRIGO NIÑO,
PRODIGY NETWORK
SPONSOR: VENERANDO
LAMELAS

48 Can glass be a fortress?

This concert hall is a collection of delicate crystals perched on the punishing Reykjavik waterfront. A collaboration with artist Olafur Eliasson, the building's south face is made of 823 "quasi-bricks"—stackable twelve-sided modules fabricated from steel and ten different types of glass that shimmer like fish scales.

But they aren't just a pretty façade—the glass bricks block noise from disturbing the performances inside. The strength of the glass combined with its structure makes this concert hall nearly impenetrable by the roiling nature around it.

Some materials have hidden powers.

Harpa Concert Hall and Conference Center. Reykjavik, Iceland
HENNING LARSEN ARCHITECTS WITH BATTERÍIĐ ARCHITECTS, RAMBØLL GROUP, AND ARTENGINEERING, AND OLAFUR ELIASSON

49 Can a light make a warehouse warm?

A warehouse is a warehouse is a warehouse, right? Well, not with a shape like this! The architects for KOP Warehouses replaced corrugated metal with corrugated transparent and translucent plastic sheets to let light in and out. The result is a simple twist on the traditional warehouse and proof that no building type is beyond innovation.

A smart architect can make a gem out of a lump of coal.

KOP Warehouses.
Puurs, Belgium
URA

50 Can a skyscraper bend over?

The new headquarters for China Central Television (CCTV) combines the entire process of TV-making—administration, production, broadcasting—into a single loop of connected activities. The building's form offers an alternative to the traditional skyscraper, encouraging collaborative activities inside, and offering an unprecedented amount of public access to China's media production system.

New public engagement creates new forms.

China Central
Television headquarters.
Beijing, China
OMA

51 Can balconies make waves?

Architectural innovation can take huge amounts of resources and time to bring to fruition. Sometimes though, the answer is in the smallest details. Underneath its exuberant form, this 82-story hotel and apartment building is really just a traditional rectangular skyscraper. When it came time to design the balconies, though, the architect became a sculptor and created curvy and changing platforms that jut out from the building up to 12 feet. From a distance, this minor alteration creates a huge spectacle— a sensual cloud floating on the Chicago skyline.

Opportunity is in the details.

Aqua Tower.
Chicago, Illinois,
United States
STUDIO GANG ARCHITECTS

52 How much does interesting cost?

A site at a busy São Paulo intersection offered architects an opportunity to create a new city landmark—all while using traditional building materials and techniques to keep costs down. Balconies arranged seemingly at random are actually a simple extension of each floor plate, granting the design complexity and character without blowing the budget.

Innovative architecture can add value to a city without adding cost.

Top Towers.
São Paulo, Brazil
KÖNIGSBERGER
VANNUCCHI ARQUITETOS

DRIVE

There are over a billion cars on Earth.
They have to go somewhere.

GAS

Sometimes it's okay just to make
something beautiful.

Gas station.
Matúškovo, Slovakia
ATELIER SAD

**No disguises necessary here.
The garage is a shapely icon that
is proud of its function.**

Parking structure for the Tyrolean Festival Erl.
Erl, Austria
KLEBOTH LINDINGER DOLLNIG

**A collage of photos taken in Venice
was translated into a four-layered design
to create a modern-day baroque
facade for this garage.**

Facade of multistory car park.
Skopje, Macedonia
PPGA ARCHITECTS

A recycled stainless-steel wrapper encloses
the first LEED-certified gas station in the US.

Helios House.
Los Angeles, California, Unites States.
OFFICE DA, JOHNSTON MARKLEE,
AND BIG - BJARKE INGELS GROUP

It's a gas station, a restaurant, a public park, and a reflecting pool. Because why shouldn't gas stations offer true amenities to travelers?

Fuel station and McDonald's.
Batumi, Georgia
GIORGI KHMALADZE ARCHITECTS

NATURE BUILDING

Nature is an increasingly influential part of building design—we are being guided by trees, rather than overwhelming them. New architecture is finding innovative methods to incorporate natural landscapes into, onto, and around buildings.

53 Can you live in a rock?

With an entry and powder room fully carved from rock, The Pierre (French for stone) is a house that celebrates the rugged landscape of its site. Stone penetrates the structure—excavated rock was even crushed and mixed into concrete flooring—and construction involved dynamite, hydraulic chippers, wire saws, and hand tools. Rather than conceal this process, marks are left exposed to celebrate it.

Maybe cavemen were on to something.

The Pierre.
San Juan Islands,
Washington,
United States
OLSON KUNDIG
ARCHITECTS

54 Can you live on a rock?

A blackened-timber cabin built over the course of a few weekends gets a leg up from a boulder; inside, the incline turns into large steps that double as seating and sleeping areas, with storage underneath.

Bumps in the road can be a good thing.

Tiny Timber
Forest Retreat.
Bohemia, Czech
Republic
UHLIK ARCHITEKTI

55 Are treehouses just for kids?

A perfect 4-meter cube suspended midway up a tree trunk is a secluded living space large enough for two people. Its mirrored glass exterior lets it all but disappear into the wooded surroundings, but birds see and avoid colliding with it thanks to a transparent ultraviolet coating.

Architecture can wear camouflage.

Treehotel.
Harads, Sweden
**THAM & VIDEGÅRD
ARKITEKTER**

56 Can architecture hug a tree?

Architects have long considered the way different bodies move through spaces. Here, a woman who is confined to a wheelchair wants her home to revolve around the garden. This redesign of two 1830s brick cottages puts nature at the center of her family activities. Even from her wheelchair, she can enjoy views of mature trees from a home that is shaped to embrace them.

Design should work for all abilities.

Tree house.
London, United
Kingdom
6A ARCHITECTS

57 Can a tree house become a house-tree?

Vietnam's tropical forests have given way to dense cities—less than .25 percent of Ho Chi Minh City is covered in trees. To help residents reconnect with nature, architects broke a house into five concrete boxes and turned the roof of each one into a giant planter. If this idea is applied to other houses in the future, the green spaces could collect and filter enough stormwater to reduce flooding citywide.

Architecture can have a green thumb.

House for Trees.
Ho Chi Minh City,
Vietnam
VO TRONG NGHIA
ARCHITECTS

58 Can new buildings learn old tricks?

The plan for this visitor center began with a motif etched on stones uncovered at the former location of a South African trading civilization. Its free-form vaults were built with a 600-year-old construction technique that is both economically and environmen-tally responsible: Local laborers made the

200,000 pressed soil tiles as part of a poverty relief program. Though it's inspired by the past, the center's design is at home in the twenty-first century, with modern geometric forms that create a new topography in the ancient setting.

Modern construction can still learn from ancient techniques.

Mapungubwe
Interpretation Centre.
Mapungubwe National
Park, Limpopo,
South Africa
PETER RICH ARCHITECTS

59 Does balanced architecture need to touch the ground?

The shape of this house may be inspired by a traditional barn, but a dramatic 50-foot cantilever that lets it hover over the ground makes it a thoroughly modern feat of architecture; exactly half of the building is floating in the air. A rigid structure that uses a heavy concrete core where the barn touches the ground makes this possible. Underneath the giant cantilever is an epic swing.

Structural innovation, and a healthy budget, make the impossible possible.

The Balancing Barn.
Suffolk, United Kingdom
MVRDV

60 Can a lawn be more than ornament?

This building is a gateway between the busy city and the silence of the botanical gardens in Brooklyn. That's why it's half building, half landscape. And its roof is more than just a pretty feature—it's connected to a system that collects stormwater to facilitate natural filtration, and serves as an icon that attracts thousands of visitors to the garden.

Responsible architecture reconnects us with nature.

Brooklyn Botanic Garden
Visitor Center.
Brooklyn, New York,
United States
WEISS/MANFREDI

61 Can grass paint a city?

This five-story-high green wall incorporates 7,600 plants from 237 species to transform a historic corner in Paris into a piece of living architecture. Beginning with a plain concrete wall, the designer installed a metal, PVC, and nonbiodegradable-felt structure that prevents damage to the building while still allowing plants to grow without soil. A built-in watering system keeps the wall healthy, allowing it to mature and change the city landscape over the course of several years.

Le Oasis d'Aboukir green wall.
Paris, France
PATRICK BLANC

Plants help keep historic architecture alive.

62 Will the city of the future be a living organism?

In these fantastical renderings (produced for the History Channel's "City of the Future" Competition), plants become power producers that harness natural energy from the sun to power an entire city. As they grow, the plants take over the city and transform it into a hybrid place: part city, part forest. At the top, a canopy of biologically enhanced plants capture energy from the sun and water from the clouds. The canopy stays low in open, suburban areas and lifts off the ground in the dense remnants of urban downtowns.

MEtreePOLIS.
(Concept)
Atlanta, Georgia,
United States
HOLLWICH KUSHNER
(HWKN)

Urban planning meets the law of the jungle.

SHELTER
FROM THE STORM

Changing climates and weather mean danger—and opportunity—for our built environments. In the face of cataclysmic natural events, architecture is often the first line of defense. But architecture can also harness nature to empower inhabitants. With hundred-year storms now coming every ten years, and energy demands growing and changing exponentially, the world needs architecture that addresses nature in all its forms.

63 Can architecture retreat from a storm?

To avoid destruction during inevitable and intensifying storms, structures built within the coastal erosion zone of the Coromandel Peninsula must be removable. This house takes the requirement as a playful design challenge. The structure functions almost like a wooden tent—a two-story shutter winches open to form a sheltering awning, and closes to protect the house in inclement weather. Perched on two sleds, the home can move to the back of its site, or across the beach and onto a barge for a total relocation.

The Earth is changing, and so should our architecture.

Hut on Sleds.
Whangapoua, New Zealand
CROSSON CLARKE
CARNACHAN ARCHITECTS

64 Can we find salvation in paper tubes?

After an earthquake devastated the New Zealand town of Christchurch, citizens were left to grieve casualties as well as the loss of their central cathedral. One architect responded with a piece of "emergency architecture"—a rapidly built cathedral made of paper tubes, shipping containers, and a lightweight polycarbonate skin. The structure could not be more simple. The result is sublime.

Rebuilding after disaster is a moment for ingenuity.

Cardboard Cathedral.
Christchurch, New
Zealand
SHIGERU BAN

65 Can green infrastructure give us super powers?

This hydroelectric dam produces 10.5 million kilowatts of energy (enough to power three thousand homes), but that is not its most impressive feat! The amazing thing about this dam is the regard the architects showed for the project's surroundings. The architects considered noise, pedestrian paths, and even the water route that fish take. The sinewy shape makes it more than simply infrastructure—it is a working public sculpture that the city cherishes.

Protection can be more than security barriers.

Hydroelectric power station. Kempten, Germany
BECKER ARCHITEKTEN

66 Can playful be practical?

Our air quality is getting worse, especially in urban areas. Who can we look to for help? Meet Wendy. Wendy maximizes her surface area to expose as much titanium-nanoparticle-coated skin to the environment as possible. Every square foot of this surface sucks CO_2 out of the air—a total equivalent to taking 250 cars off of the road. The best part of Wendy is that she has a personality—she is big and blue and spiky, and she shoots out jets of water, and she has a name. The project was as much a social experiment as it was an ecological experiment.

Architecture can have personality *and* help the Earth.

Wendy: 2012 MoMA/PS1 Young Architects Program winner. Queens, New York, United States
HOLLWICH KUSHNER (HWKN)

67 Can we design for disaster?

In an area that was swampland two hundred years ago, the coastal playgrounds of Hunter's Point are prone to flooding in storms. The architects worked with the engineering team to anticipate this—the sunken oval playing field is designed to flood and act as a buffer for the rest of the park and the neighborhood beyond. It is a layered strategy that purposefully sacrifices playing fields in the event of a storm, rather than harder-to-replace infrastructure and houses.

Architecture helps us prioritize during a disaster.

Hunter's Point South Park.
Queens, New York, United States
THOMAS BALSLEY ASSOCIATES
AND WEISS/MANFREDI

68 Can architecture save us from the apocalypse?

Think of this as a safety deposit box for the world's seeds. Inside a mountain on a remote island halfway between Norway and the North Pole, this state-of-the-art storage facility provides what scientists believe is a failsafe way to protect food crops in the event of manmade or natural disaster. Built under thick rock and permafrost, the collection of millions of "backup" seed samples can remain frozen even in a power outage, securing the seed supply for centuries.

Give peas a chance.

Svalbard Global
Seed Vault.
Longyearbyen, Norway
BARLINDHAUGKONSERNET

69 Can architecture be a sponge?

New York has had some serious recovery work to do since Hurricane Sandy devastated its coastal neighborhoods in 2012. Six design teams have been chosen to develop innovative plans to protect the region from future storms. Plans range from huge berms that will protect the East River Park community from storm surges—while providing new recreational space—to green infrastructure that will store excess water and prevent flooding. Pictured here is the Big U, a series of green berms and landscapes to absorb storm surges.

Bad things can inspire us to do good.

The Big U:
Rebuild by Design
competition.
(Concept)
New York, New York,
United States
BIG TEAM, INTERBORO
TEAM, MIT CAU + ZUS
+ URBANISTEN, OMA,
PENNDESIGN/OLIN, AND
SCAPE / LANDSCAPE
ARCHITECTURE

70 How many ways can a roof serve a building?

With temperatures on the rise, roofs must be enlisted in the fight against climate change. In the spirit of technological advancement, this building will have what SHoP Architects calls an "Energy Blanket"—a roofscape designed to both collect and conserve energy using a range of innovative techniques, including solar panels, a water collection and recycling system, and huge

overhangs to shade the building's interiors.
The mission of this 270,000-square-foot
research facility is to support innovation and
entrepreneurship in Botswana. It includes a
data center, engineering floors, and an HIV
research lab run by an international consortium.

Even incubators need shade.

Botswana
Innovation Hub.
Gaborone, Botswana
SHOP ARCHITECTS

SHRINK

By 2050, more than 80 percent of the world's people will live in cities.
That means that every square foot counts.

How can we think smaller?

A polyester shell encloses an egglike multifunctional space. It includes a bathroom, kitchen, and niches for sleeping and storage. When the nose is opened, the whole structure becomes a porch.

Blob VB3.
Mechelen, Belgium
DMVA ARCHITECTEN

This 914-square-foot transparent house is inspired by the concept of living in a tree, with twenty-one different floors at various heights to allow its owners never-ending variety.

House NA.
Tokyo, Japan
SOU FUJIMOTO ARCHITECTS

This 19-square-meter house has four rooms and was built for a quarter of the price of a similarly sized apartment in the same area.

Boxhome.
Oslo, Norway
RINTALA EGGERTSSON ARCHITECTS

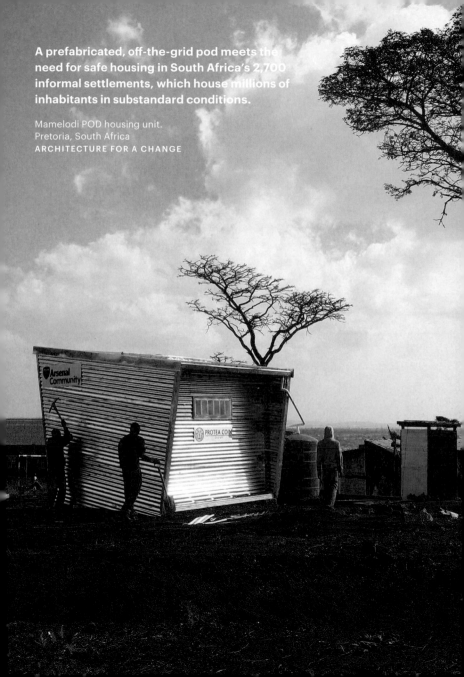

A prefabricated, off-the-grid pod meets the need for safe housing in South Africa's 2,700 informal settlements, which house millions of inhabitants in substandard conditions.

Mamelodi POD housing unit.
Pretoria, South Africa
ARCHITECTURE FOR A CHANGE

Part art installation, part artist's residence, this house measures 28 inches at its narrowest and four feet at its widest point.

Keret House.
Warsaw, Poland
JAKUB SZCZĘSNY

A tiny office wedged like a barnacle between two larger buildings allows traffic to flow beneath.

Parasite Office.
Moscow, Russia
ZA BOR ARCHITECTS

SOCIAL CATALYSTS

Cities are living organisms—without the right cultivation, they wither and die. Architecture has the power to stitch individuals into a community and energize forgotten corners of our urban fabric. Communities use architecture to plant a flag and rally together. Catalysts can be youth centers, religious buildings, libraries, and even beehives, but regardless of its use, architecture is a potent tool for encouraging the act of community.

71 Would you let your kids play in a wasteland?

Postindustrial wastelands don't always spark enthusiasm from local communities, but this project transformed a defunct warehouse and brownfield (land previously used for industry) into a public park and performance space with an amphitheater that rises like a wave from a wooden boardwalk. Now, this economically strained Virginia rail town has a new sense of pride that is rooted in nature, rather than industrial decay.

Landscape architecture can transform brown to green.

Smith Creek Park.
Clifton Forge, Virginia,
United States
DESIGN/BUILDLAB
AT VIRGINIA TECH

72 Can you swim in poop?

New York City is surrounded by water, but you wouldn't want to swim there—the city drains effluent directly into its rivers every time it rains. That's all going to change thanks to a crowdfunded initiative to build the world's first water-filtering floating pool. This giant Brita-esque pool will filter up to a half million gallons of river water each day, making the rivers cleaner over time and creating a much-needed public amenity that will reconnect us to the urban waterfront.

It's your city. You should be able to use it.

Plus POOL initiative.
(Concept)
New York, New York,
United States
FAMILY AND PLAYLAB

73 Can honeybees fight blight?

A colony of honeybees that had taken up residence in an abandoned building needed to be relocated. So a group of local architecture students designed them a new home in a 22-foot-tall honeycomb-shaped tower with perforated steel panels made to protect the hive from wind and weather. Inside, a cypress wood box with a glass bottom lets visitors see the bees at work from below. The new habitat is an educational opportunity for children and adults alike, who get to see the economic and environmental regeneration happening throughout this Buffalo neighborhood.

Underused urban areas can become hives of activity.

Hive City: Elevator B. Buffalo, New York, United States
UNIVERSITY AT BUFFALO SCHOOL AT ARCHITECTURE AND PLANNING

74 Can architecture feed a community?

Sitting atop a former twentieth-century factory, a 40,000-square-foot field is the largest rooftop soil farm in the United States. Part of a local for-profit initiative that now spans two rooftops in New York City, the gardens produce more than 50,000 pounds of organic produce each year for residents. It's local, organic, and takes advantage of a structure that was sitting unused for decades.

Join the roof-to-table movement.

Brooklyn Grange. Queens, New York, United States
BROMLEY CALDARI ARCHITECTS

75 Can paint unite a city?

This public artwork project began in 2010 as a collaboration between Dutch artists Jeroen Koolhaas and Dre Urhahn and a local team in Rio de Janeiro's Santa Marta favela—favelas are Brazilian slums or shantytowns—turning it into a more vibrant, appealing place. Since then, they have spread their movement across the

world, transforming a dilapidated area in North
Philadelphia and working with communities
in Curaçao and elsewhere to alter depressed
public spaces in ways that will attract positive
attention and economic impulses.

Positive change can come in a few cans
of paint.

Favela Painting Project.
Rio de Janeiro, Brazil
HAAS&HAHN

76 Can color change your morning commute?

Just a few meters from one of Bratislava's historic squares, a dimly lit bus terminal sat neglected for years. To empower commuters, architects enlisted the local community to paint 1,000 square meters of pavement with green road paint. Two years later, they pushed the low-cost design intervention further with a crowdsourced lighting unit that was produced and installed with 4,000 meters of white packing tape. The resulting space is bright, cheery and a far cry from the drab station it once was.

An uplifting public space doesn't have to be expensive, but it does have to be smart.

Bus terminal under the bridge.
Bratislava, Slovakia
VALLO SADOVSKY ARCHITECTS

77 Can design help women thrive?

The nonprofit organization Women for Women International teaches war survivors marketable skills, empowering them to remake their communities. A designer collaborated with the organization to create a community center with an inviting public plaza—a meeting place designed to bridge the gap between urban buyers and rural farmers. The facility's sustainable systems are maintained by the women who live nearby, ensuring a strong local network that can support the community for future generations.

Architecture helps rebuild lives.

Women's Opportunity Center.
Kayonza, Rwanda
SHARON DAVIS DESIGN

78 Can opera empower a village?

In 2009, Burkinabé architect **Francis Kéré** teamed up with the late German film and theater director Christoph Schlingensief to bring an opera house to the rural area of Laongo. The two embarked on an incredible journey to heighten the cultural identity of the region, which was already the center of African film and theater. Still in progress, this "opera house for Africa" and educational center is already bringing together local residents and local materials to create beautiful music on a 30-acre campus that includes a five-hundred-student school and a health center.

A creative community is its own oasis.

Opera Village.
Laongo, Burkina Faso
KÉRÉ ARCHITECTURE

79 Can a garden shed unite a community?

A humble garden shed takes on a fantastic form to avoid casting shadows on nearby garden plots. Made of chemical-free materials, the building creates a shaded meeting space, while the charred cedar siding doubles as a chalkboard wall for messages and tips. The herringbone pattern of the wooden slats filter light into the interior while creating a trellis for seasonal vines.

Architecture is like gardening: You reap what you sow.

Woodlands Community Garden shed. Vancouver, Canada
BRENDAN CALLANDER, JASON PIELAK, AND STELLA CHEUNG-BOYLAND

80 Can small housing be great housing?

Demographers predict that New York will add at least 1 million more residents by 2040— and many of these are expected to be one- or two-person middle-income households that won't qualify for city subsidies or financing. Sponsored by the mayor's office, the adAPT NYC competition sought new housing options for this growing population. This winning plan uses a solution of modular housing units that can be stacked to create fifty-five new microunits sized to 250 square feet. The concept can be adapted to many different locations, allowing city developers to meet the changing needs of citizens as quickly as cities grow.

Cities need homes for teachers and nurses, too.

My Micro NY: adAPT NYC competition winner. (Concept)
NARCHITECTS

81 Can architecture be crowdsourced and crowdfunded?

Mi Ciudad Ideal (My Ideal City) is an effort to crowdsource and document citizens' wishes for the future of their city and, eventually, to crowdfund them. Launched in Bogotá, Colombia, the program has already drawn participation from more than 130,000 residents. This new "bottom-up" approach to urban planning is well-suited to Latin American cities, where a huge boom in the number of middle-class citizens is requiring innovative solutions. The first example of this effort is BD Bacatá, a skyscraper created by Prodigy Network and sponsored by BD Promotores, that holds the world record in crowdfunding. It's a huge step in citizen participation and investment in a city's evolving needs.

130,000 heads are better than one.

Downtown Bogotá
revitalization scenario
from the My Ideal
City initiative.
(Concept)
Bogotá, Colombia
WINKA DUBBELDAM,
ARCHI-TECHTONICS

82 What happens when architecture keeps score?

In less than six months, architects of this Nike-funded football training facility created a place where twenty thousand footballers of all ages can play throughout the year. The first of its kind in Africa, the facility is designed to have an open feeling, but crime is a daily reality in this Johannesburg township. The building's transparency welcomes the community with invisible security at all times. The center has limited access points, and its wooden louver facade creates a tight perimeter outside, while huge expanses of glass face inward, toward the protected playing field at the center of the complex. Architects even commissioned the local artist Kronk to turn the security fence into a site-specific artwork, masking its true purpose.

Architecture should protect and serve.

Football Training Centre.
Soweto, South Africa
RURAL/URBAN/FANTASY
PROJECT

83 Can a library be a lighthouse?

The new library of Alexandria is built on roughly the same site as the library founded by Alexander the Great 2,300 years ago, but the similarities end there. The building is composed of a giant slanted circle 160 meters in diameter. The glazed roof lets sunlight in at optimum levels to protect the books and wash the space with natural illumination. Like many modern libraries, the institution has expanded its mission beyond just books (though it can house up to 8 million of those too, and claims to have the world's largest reading room). With a planetarium, four museums, an information science school, and conservation facilities, the library has a new, more important role in the community than ever before.

A new roof can give an ancient library new life.

Bibliotheca Alexandrina.
Alexandria, Egypt
SNØHETTA

84 Can you get married in a parking garage?

There are over 105 million commercial parking spaces in the United States, and they are not always full. This Miami Beach parking garage creates a civic amenity out of its three hundred parking spaces. They can be repurposed when empty, thanks to super-high ceilings and amazing views. When the cars are gone, the building is used for yoga in the morning and is rented out for events at night.

Inefficient parking can create great public infrastructure.

1111 Lincoln Road.
Miami Beach, Florida,
United States
HERZOG & DE MEURON

85 Can a library be relevant in the digital age?

At the Seattle public library, the architects considered the way we consume media in a digital age and turned the library into a relevant public amenity by redefining it as an institution dedicated to more than just books. All forms of media—new and old— are represented here. They even redesigned the Dewey decimal system to make the place more intuitive and welcoming. The building's shape is a direct result of this rearrangement.

Libraries still have a lot to learn.

Seattle Central Library.
Seattle, Washington,
United States
OMA + LMN

86 Can you sunbathe underground?

Manhattan's High Line proved that an elevated rail line could have a second life as a vibrant public space. Now, a project called The Lowline aims to convert an unused trolley terminal into a subterranean hub for year-round events and activities. The plan uses a cutting-edge solar technology called a "remote skylight" to collect sunlight and direct it underground, allowing plants, and people, to thrive in a previously uninhabitable space.

As urban spaces become scarce, we appreciate them more.

The Lowline.
(Concept)
New York, New York,
United States
RAAD STUDIO

87 Can flipping a switch enliven a neighborhood?

This light and slender building at Paris Diderot University neighbors a hulking academic building next door. The new building faces a public square and acts as a bright gravitational counterpoint to the existing building. The open first floor beckons visitors in, and at night the entire building becomes a place-making icon for the university.

Opposites attract.

M3A2 Cultural and
Community Tower.
Paris, France
ANTONINI DARMON
ARCHITECTES

FAST
FORWARD

We have been taught to expect the same thing from buildings over and over again: inert boxes made of concrete, steel, and glass. But in the near future, buildings will be wildly different than anything we experience today. This change begins with technology impacting our building materials, because the way we build impacts what we build. From 3-D printed houses to mushroom bricks, today's emerging technologies look beyond the hammer and nail to imagine a new way of constructing.

88   Can a building clean the air?

Welcome to the age of smog-eating architecture. Slated to make its debut at the 2015 Milan Expo, a 13,000-square-meter building will become an air purifier for the city, with a concrete facade that absorbs airborne pollutants and converts them into harmless salts that are then washed away by the rain.

Architecture helps us breathe easy.

Italian Pavilion.
Milan, Italy
NEMESI & PARTNERS

89   Can we print a house?

The 3D Print Canal House is an exhibition and experimentation site that remakes the typical Dutch canal house into a 3-D-printed home for the twenty-first century. The process of making turns digital files into physical building blocks using a KamerMaker, a large-scale version of a desktop printer. This makes it possible for the designers to create detailed components in a local style. The house is produced on-site, so there are no material transportation costs, and the potential for local manufacturing is high—meaning cities may no longer have to seek cheap building materials from far away as 3-D printing technology takes hold at the local level.

Knowledge comes from making.

3D Print Canal House.
(Concept)
Amsterdam, Netherlands
DUS ARCHITECTS

90 Can mushrooms replace stone?

These bricks are made of mushrooms. Mushrooms! The "bio-bricks" were grown inside of reflective trays made out of a mirrored film. These reflective containers were later used at the top of the tower to bounce daylight into the structure and the space around it. The tower's shape is designed to be efficient, too, cooling itself by pushing hot air out at the top. In contrast to the energy-gobbling skyscrapers on New York City's skyline, Hy-Fi offers a thought-provoking glimpse of the future. Hope you like mushrooms.

We can grow the future.

Hy-Fi: 2014 MoMA/ PS1 Young Architects Program winner. Queens, New York, United States
THE LIVING

91 Can worms replace workers?

Silk doesn't seem like the sturdiest building material, but a group at MIT turned to 6,500 live silkworms to build a structure that connects nature with technology in a whole new way. They programmed a robotic arm to create a framework across a metal scaffold that gave the silkworms a roadmap to follow. When the worms were let loose on the structure, they responded to light, heat, and geometry, producing patterns that were a reflection of their environment. The resulting dome could inspire researchers to design and make man-made fiber structures never before imagined.

Architecture can imitate the beautiful efficiency of nature.

Silk Pavilion.
Cambridge, Massachusetts,
United States
MIT MEDIA LAB MEDIATED
MATTER GROUP

92 Can metal breathe?

The outside of a building, its skin, should be more similar to human skin—dynamic and responsive to the environment. That's the idea behind smart thermo-bimetal. Because it is made of two strips of different metals that respond differently to heat, this experimental building material requires no controls or energy to react to changes in temperature. When installed, its reactive property allows the system to ventilate on hot days, while shading it at the same time.

Humans breathe—so should our buildings.

Bloom.
(Concept)
DORIS KIM SUNG

93 What if houses were made of meat?

In the future you will be able to live inside a pig—sort of. No animals are harmed in the creation of Meat Habitat, a to-scale model of a house made with meat cells grown in a lab. The concept is a glimpse at replacing traditional building materials with pig cells that are 3-D-printed to create full-size architecture. And don't worry about preservatives. The skin is grown with sodium benzoate to kill yeasts, bacteria, and fungi—it will last longer than a Twinkie in its cellophane wrapper.

We could grow our houses by rethinking material structures.

In Vitro Meat Habitat.
(Concept)
MITCHELL JOACHIM OF
TERREFORM ONE

94 Can bacteria be your architect?

A 6,000-kilometer-long inhabitable wall in the Sahara Desert isn't built—it is grown, with the help of a bacteria that turns sand into sandstone. This is the concept behind Dune, a naturally generated sand structure that relies on a biological reaction: The sandstone is grown with the help of *Bacillus pasteurii*, a bacterial microorganism found in marshes and wetlands. Once introduced, the bacteria might be able to create a structurally sound and livable structure in less than a week, opening new possibilities for rapidly deployable refugee housing in the desert.

The desert is a living place.

Dune.
(Concept)
Sahara Desert, North Africa
MAGNUS LARSSON

95 Can architecture go wiki?

WikiHouse is a small experiment with a big idea: That regular people (read: not architects) can build a house anywhere with minimal tools and training. The open source construction system makes it possible for anyone to design, share, download, and "print" (with a CNC mill) quickly buildable houses from sheet materials like plywood that are low-cost but also suited to local needs. Continuously under development, solutions in the works include post-earthquake housing and a factory in one of Rio's favelas.

Design for the 100 percent.

WikiHouse.
(Concept)
ALASTAIR PARVIN

96 Can a building have reflexes?

The attention-grabbing Media-ITC building was designed as a collaborative space for the advancement of new technology. Its outer walls reflect this mission, with a translucent skin of temperature-regulating inflatable bubbles. Sensors automatically inflate the shading cushions to block light and reduce cooling costs on hot days, or deflate to let in more light on cloudy days.

Architecture made of air can help keep us cool.

Media-ITC.
Barcelona, Spain
ENRIC RUIZ-GELI/CLOUD 9

97 What if drones carried bricks, not missiles?

Flight Assembled Architecture is an installation built by flying robots. To build the 6-meter-high structure, a group of four-bladed helicopters carried fifteen hundred foam bricks and placed them based on digital design data that dynamically controls their behavior. This visionary approach to building is the result of a collaboration between architects Gramazio & Kohler and inventor Raffaello D'Andrea, who belong to a new generation of architects seeking to push the limits of digital design and fabrication.

No cranes. No ladders. No limits.

Flight Assembled
Architecture.
(Concept)
Orléans, France
GRAMAZIO & KOHLER AND
RAFFAELLO D'ANDREA

98 Can a skyscraper be built in a day?

Building a skyscraper used to take years. But a group in China is changing everything we know about construction, building a fifteen-story hotel in six days, then a thirty-story hotel in just over two weeks. The secret is prefabrication: Large sections of the building were assembled in a factory, eliminating waste and delays at the building site. According to the China Academy of Building Research, the tower is five times more earthquake-resistant than a similar one built with traditional methods.

Even if buildings can happen in the blink of an eye, they should still stand the test of time.

T30 Hotel.
Hunan Province, China
BROAD GROUP

99   Can skyscrapers be made of wood?

The idea of a wooden skyscraper raises eyebrows—and a lot of questions: Can it stand up in an earthquake? What if it catches fire? But this design competition winner proposes a thirty-four-story wooden skyscraper that would have the safety attributes of steel or concrete, with less construction waste and better acoustics than traditional high rises. The idea is more than speculation; Sweden's largest housing association plans to complete the tower by 2023.

New ideas can grow on trees.

HSB Stockholm competition winner. (Concept)
Stockholm, Sweden
BERG | C.F. MØLLER AND DINELLJOHANSSON

100 What if a cow built your house?

To create this experimental structure, cleverly named The Truffle, a group of architects dug a hole, packed it with hay, and then poured concrete around it. After the concrete dried, a calf named Paulina moved in, eating the hay for a year and hollowing out a small cave in the process—all that was left in the end was the scratches and imprints of how the place was made. It is a fantastically hideous little building that became the most sublime place to watch a Spanish sunset. It's also a true melding of the most important tenets of future building: reliance on known techniques, forward-thinking environmentalism, whimsy, and brilliant simplicity. Moo.

The future of architecture will surprise you.

The Truffle.
Laxe, Spain
ENSAMBLE STUDIO

After journeying through these one hundred buildings, hopefully it's clear that there is no perfect, universal solution for the future of architecture. All across the globe, architects are eagerly working with clients and skilled builders to design unique buildings, tailored to changing environmental and social needs. They are pushing the envelope, barreling towards the unknowable future. And they need your help.

Don't be a bystander and let architecture simply *happen* to you. Find an architect. Study up on the latest ideas in architecture. Talk with the people designing the places where you spend your time. Talk with your neighbors, coworkers, friends, and family, and together, insist on good architecture.

Remember: Architecture doesn't just represent your community— it shapes your society. If you ask architecture to work for you, and to reflect the priorities of your community and the Earth, you will be amazed by the possibilities architecture can bring to every aspect of your life.

Happy building!

PHOTO CREDITS

1 Anthony Dubber and James Morris

2 Marc Lins Photography

3 diephotodesigner, Reiulf Ramstad Arkitekter

4 diephotodesigner, courtesy of Snøhetta

5 Iwan Baan

6 Minarc (Tryggvi Thorsteinsson, Erla Dögg Ingjaldsdóttir)

7 Luis García

8 Mika Huisman

9 Roland Halbe

10 © Foster + Partners / ESA

11 Roos Aldershoff Fotografie

12 Lv Hengzhong

13 Jeff Goldberg / Esto

14 Peter Clarke

15 Morris Adjmi Architects

16 Heatherwick Studio

17 Johannes Arlt, laif / Redux

18 Roland Halbe

19 Brenchley Architects / Elizabeth Allnut Photography

20 Fernando Alda David Franck

21 Tamás Bujnovszky

22 LOT-EK

23 Bernardes + Jacobsen

24 Iwan Baan

25 A2arquitectos

26 Ricardo Oliveira Alves

27 Thomas Ibsen

28 Reversible Destiny Foundation

29 Turner Brooks Architect

30 Jan Glasmeier

31 Fernando Guerra FG+SG

POP-UP

BULGARI Abu Dhabi Art Pavilion
NANA

PDU (Portable Dining Unit)
Cesar Rubio, courtesy of EDG Interior Architecture + Design

Floatastic
Net Martin Studio, B. Lapolla & Mahdi Alibakhshian

Head in the Clouds
Chuck Choi

Drift Pavilion for Design Miami/2012
Markus Haugg

32 Marcus Buck

33 Lucerne Festival Ark Nova 2013

34 Hufton + Crow

35 Robert Polidori

36 Iwan Baan

37 Duccio Malagamba

38 left image: Imre Solt, right image: Torsten Seidel

39 Craft Arquitectos

40 Rafael Gamo

41 Marco Boella, courtesy of JDS Architects

42 Nikolaos Zachariadis and SPLITTERWERK

43 Timothy Hursley

44 Studio Guilherme Torres

45 Iwan Baan

46 Scagliola Brakkee

47 BIG - Bjarke Ingels Group

AUTHOR THANKS

This book would not have been possible without the amazing work of Jennifer Krichels, who smiled all the way from Building 1 to Building 100. Special thanks to Matthias Hollwich, and to the teams at TED and at Architizer, especially Catherine Finsness, Siddharth Saxena and Luna Bernfest. To Chris Barley, the most patient speaking coach in the world—none of this would have been possible without your support. Thanks to the photographers for capturing all of this amazing work. Finally, thanks to the architects and their clients for designing and building such a magnificent group of buildings.

ABOUT THE AUTHOR

MARC KUSHNER is a practicing architect who splits his time between designing buildings at HWKN, the architecture firm he cofounded, and amassing the world's architecture on the website he runs, Architizer.com. Both have the same mission: to reconnect the public with architecture.

Kushner's core belief is that architecture touches everyone—and everyone is a fan of architecture—even if they don't know it yet. New forms of media empower people to shape the built environment, and that means better buildings that make better cities that make a better world.

Marc Kushner spoke at the TED Conference in 2014. His TED Talk, available for free at TED.com, was the inspiration for *The Future of Architecture in 100 Buildings.*

PHOTO: JAMES DUNCAN DAVIDSON / TED

RELATED TALKS ON TED.COM

Michael Green: *Why We Should Build Wooden Skyscrapers*
go.ted.com/Green

Building a skyscraper? Forget about steel and concrete, says architect Michael Green, and build it out of wood. Green explains that it's not only possible to build safe wooden structures up to thirty stories tall (and, he hopes, higher), it's also necessary.

Alastair Parvin: *Architecture for the People by the People*
go.ted.com/Parvin

What if regular citizens could design and build their own houses? The concept is at the heart of WikiHouse, an open source construction kit that means just about anyone can build a house, anywhere.

Thomas Heatherwick: *Building the Seed Cathedral*
go.ted.com/Heatherwick

A showcase of five recent projects featuring ingenious bio-inspired designs. Some are remakes of the ordinary—a bus, a bridge, a power station—and one is an extraordinary pavilion, the Seed Cathedral, a celebration of growth and light

Bjarke Ingels: *Building With Nature*
go.ted.com/Ingels

Danish architect Bjarke Ingels rockets through photo/video-mingled stories of his eco-flashy designs. His buildings not only look like nature—they act like nature: blocking the wind, collecting solar energy—and creating stunning views.

ABOUT TED BOOKS

TED Books are small books about big ideas. They're short enough to read in a single sitting, but long enough to delve deep into a topic. The wide-ranging series covers everything from architecture to business, space travel to love, and is perfect for anyone with a curious mind and an expansive love of learning.

Each TED Book is paired with a related TED Talk, available online at TED.com. The books pick up where the talks leave off. An eighteen-minute speech can plant a seed or spark the imagination, but many talks create a need to go deeper, to learn more, to tell a longer story. TED Books fills this need.

COMING SOON

Follow Your Gut: The Enormous Impact of Tiny Microbes by Rob Knight with Brendan Buhler

In this groundbreaking book, scientist Rob Knight reveals how the microscopic life within our bodies—particularly within our intestines—has an astonishing impact on our lives. Your health, mood, sleep patterns, eating preferences, and more can all be traced in part to the tiny creatures that live on and inside of us.

ABOUT TED

TED is a nonprofit devoted to spreading ideas, usually in the form of short, powerful talks (eighteen minutes or less) but also through books, animation, radio programs, and events. TED began in 1984 as a conference where Technology, Entertainment, and Design converged, and today covers almost every topic — from science to business to global issues — in more than one hundred languages.

TED is a global community, welcoming people from every discipline and culture who seek a deeper understanding of the world. We believe passionately in the power of ideas to change attitudes, lives, and, ultimately, our future. On TED.com, we're building a clearinghouse of free knowledge from the world's most inspired thinkers — and a community of curious souls to engage with ideas and each other. Our annual flagship conference convenes thought leaders from all fields to exchange ideas. Our TEDx program allows communities worldwide to host their own independent, local events, all year long. And our Open Translation Project ensures these ideas can move across borders.

In fact, everything we do — from the TED Radio Hour to the projects sparked by the TED Prize, from TEDx events to the TED-Ed lesson series — is driven by this goal: How can we best spread great ideas?

TED is owned by a nonprofit, nonpartisan foundation.